ASPECTS OF WAR

Edited by

Steph Park-Pirie

First published in Great Britain in 2004 by
POETRY NOW
Remus House,
Coltsfoot Drive,
Peterborough, PE2 9JX
Telephone (01733) 898101
Fax (01733) 313524

SB ISBN 1 84460 838 7

FOREWORD

Although we are a nation of poets we are accused of not reading poetry, or buying poetry books. After many years of listening to the incessant gripes of poetry publishers, I can only assume that the books they publish, in general, are books that most people do not want to read.

Poetry should not be obscure, introverted, and as cryptic as a crossword puzzle: it is the poet's duty to reach out and embrace the world.

The world owes the poet nothing and we should not be expected to dig and delve into a rambling discourse searching for some inner meaning.

The reason we write poetry (and almost all of us do) is because we want to communicate: an ideal; an idea; or a specific feeling. Poetry is as essential in communication, as a letter; a radio; a telephone, and the main criterion for selecting the poems in this anthology is very simple: they communicate.

CONTENTS

THE FINAL DRINK

After a hard week's graft
The men walked to the pub
Building up an appetite
For their Sunday lunchtime grub.
Suddenly they came
Flying not much higher than the waves
People ran for cover
Hiding in the Hastings' caves
Bombs started falling
Killing rich and poor
The pub with the men in
Now stands no more
We remember the stench
We remember the fear
We'll always remember the men
Having their Sunday lunchtime beer.

Gillian Maynard

A Father's Love

War on the home front is what springs to mind
as he sits on a bench and ponders awhile.
Have you seen this old man as he goes on his way?
What does he do each and every day?
His age I don't know but he looks very old,
I wonder if you've heard the stories he's told.
There are stories of times so long, long ago
when he was a boy in the war you know,
he tells of the soldiers who went off to fight
and his dad leaving home in the middle of the night
of him never returning from World War I
where he went off to fight holding only a gun
of himself growing up and meeting new friends,
having small fights and making amends
of him getting a job and having the crack
but his one wish in life was to have his dad back
now that my friend was not to be
for his dad fought the war so his son could be free.
And later in life how he met his dear wife
who promised to love him all of her life
how she bore him three sons and a beautiful daughter
and the days they shared filled with fun and laughter
but then it happened what all men feared,
another war was declared,
he heard Churchill say on the radio that night
we will not run away, we will stand and fight,
so history repeated itself once more
he took up his gun and pulled out the door
he waved goodbye to his family and friends
and said to his sons on ye I depend
take care of your mother and sister too
and never forget I do love you
how he fought brave and hard and stood by his men
and even helped take out Hitler the evil one then

and of when the war ended he headed for home
injured and hurt but never alone
for by his side was a guiding hand
of one other man who fought for his land
a friend who had helped him through thick and thin
always at hand through everything
a man who stood up ever so tall,
who made the whole world look so very small,
how he walked with him right up to his home
and said, 'My dear son, you have not been alone.
My time with you it has to end
but I've brought you home to your family and friends.'
How he quickly turned to see whose arm he'd had,
he knew there and then his friend was his dad.
This figure who'd stood by his side to fight
had vanished like dust in the mist of the night.

Maureen O'Halloran

DOODLEBUG AWAKENING (1944)
(Dedicated to the memory of Keith and Betty de Berry)

The racketty motor spluttered loud
flying low with fearsome drone
echoing beneath blanket cloud,
spreading fear in many a home.

Worse still, the noise fell silent.
Who knows where that missile would fall?
Sign of enemy's evil intent
designed to kill or frighten all.

That night we lay in shored-up room
with neighbours, sleeping as we could.
There came a crashing awful boom
as flying bomb fell in nearby wood.

It struck a tree and tore it down,
blast damaging a dozen homes.
Huddled together, with worried frown,
hair full of dust, defying combs!

The rumbling stopped. We're all OK.
Soon, comes a knock on the front door,
'Is it really still there?' we say.
Enter rescue squad to assess the score.

Those cheerful men tramp through the dust
plus the chief warden of the ARP.
For him this visit is a must -
he's also the vicar - O K de B!

No one is hurt, we're glad to say.
The rubble and glass is not too bad.
We'll live to see another day,
though losing belongings is sad.

The vicar issues his invitation -
the vicarage basement is apparently free.
So quickly we make our reservation.
Will he bring us all our morning tea?

Three weeks or so we sheltered there
alongside the boiler and supply of coal.
Respite after a nasty scare,
we couldn't have found a nicer hole!

Betty made welcome to her kitchen fare,
as several made breakfast as usual.
So open to all who sojourned there,
her gracious spirit more then dutiful.

I feared in those weeks that OK de B,
armed with his known godly zeal,
would seize every chance to evangelise me.
Instead, he scarce sat down for a meal!

Soon we're rehoused in a new street,
fear of 'religion' was distant it seemed,
then came the curate with story so neat
seeking my help with the youth soccer team.

Strange, then, that this kindly ploy
for me should be so hard to resist,
and captured forever the heart of a boy
who couldn't say, 'Invitation dismissed!'

To cut this reminiscence short;
in a year, for God, this youth was won.
After some stress of heart and thought
he found a saviour in God's own Son.

Would I be Christian if no bomb fell?
Should I thank Hitler for making it so?
Not so. The enemy was giving us hell
but, 'things work together for good', now I know.

So thanks to God who makes all things new,
and for the gospel that opened a door.
Thanks for the work of His servants true
whose life continues with Christ evermore.

Jo Allen

AT HOME IN THE SECOND WORLD WAR

The siren went at ten to four,
We quickly made our way to the door;
Across the field to trenches deep,
We raced as fast as legs would leap.

The clouds all filled with fire and smoke,
For Sherborne town this was no joke;
The German planes their bombs dropped free,
Our fighter planes made Germans flee.

The Home Guard did their duties well,
Each night at local station dwell;
All armed with shotguns, rifles too,
Then dear old Bren gun came on view.

When siren screeched out in the night,
Dear Mum in panic, full of fright;
If Dad at home to shelter we went,
If Mum alone, under table we bent.

A girl next door from London came,
Escape the Blitz with bombers to blame;
Our new found friends soon learnt our ways,
They loved the country, new things each day.

Our windows all blacked out at night,
If chink of light then warden bites;
The help and comradeship was great,
We learned and shared as life-long mates.

With peace declared, festivities start,
The joy and revels came from heart;
Through six long years all news of war,
Left so much sadness, but hopes did soar.

John Paulley

MEMORIES OF A WARTIME CHILDHOOD

Did you go to school in the forties,
In the days of World War II?
Then you will remember those gas masks,
Rationing and making do.
Practising for those daytime air raids,
As quickly and silently we filed
Into dank, brick built shelters,
And squashed in, next to some unseen child.

We recited tables twice over,
To twelve and then back again,
Pounds and ounces, yards, feet and inches,
Pounds, shillings and pence; and then
Set free to scamper round the playground,
Roll marbles or skip with a rope,
We exorcised fears all around us
And that exercise helped us to cope.

One Christmas my sister was given
A smart box to put her mask in.
But my gas mask had to be carried
In an old national dried milk tin.
My dad fixed on a rope handle
And painted the outside all black.
Then twice a day it was carried
Down the hill to my school and then back.

In autumn we saved all our coupons
For toffees and sweets at Yule.
All coke and coal was strictly rationed,
Mum had to store up winter fuel.
Trees for Christmas could not be grown then,
The land was needed for food,
But two wooden hoops linked together,
Wrapped in paper, were almost as good.

Times must have been hard for my parents,
But our home was filled with love.
Dear Mum and Dad both worked together,
And prayed to our Father above.
We were some of the lucky children
Who survived all the hardships of war.
We must pass on the Christmas message
Of peace, love and hope for evermore.

Doreen Lawrence

A PEACE-FILLED PRIDE

'My grandfather nearly died . . .'
but won't speak of it now.
How the timber collapsed his lung,
and the sun was lost behind a muddy cloud.

And, mine, was at the front.
Shot in the leg for his trouble.
Hobbling after the war, and no good.
His stories muddled.

I'm proud Grandad was a gunner -
shelled villages to rubble.
Took names and ranks and souvenirs,
'cause they all had it coming.

Some put the lights in London out.
Never picked up a gun.
Mine-planned battles every Wednesday night at nine.
But the battles didn't come.

Kevin Hayhoe

JUST ANOTHER LONDON DAY

The street was empty, silence reigned
Rubble, dust and desolation.
The broken remains of a once proud nation
London was coping so they claimed.

Every night the bombs now fell
And lit the sky like mayday flairs.
God's ears were clogged with desperate prayers
At every toll of the warning bell.

By morning all fires had long burned out.
Many died in their own beds.
Crushed by the roof above their heads,
Without a gasp or muffled shout.

Shattered glass like shattered love,
Lay on a canvas of dirt and mud.
Laced with fresh and sticky blood,
Carnage reaped from high above.

Yet something stirred, a girl appeared,
With sunken eyes and pale face.
Who walked with courage and with grace,
To the bombed outhouse where she was reared.

Within two hours the streets were teeming,
With men in ties and pinstripe suits.
And market stalls of home-grown fruits,
One may have thought they were dreaming.

But this was London, this was pride,
Of a people whose spirit will never die.
As they fought the invaders from the sky,
Their heroism turned the tide.

Tom Bohills

THE POPPIES

Every time a plane flies overhead, I still tense -
Afraid of what it once meant.
Lying down in the shelter, hour after hour,
Whilst the fear was immense.

Iron railings still make me remember the war,
Changed into munitions in the factories roar!
Ever resourceful, 'make-do-and-mend',
Spirits lifted, normal life at an end.

An old wireless sends my memory back.
Trying to hear the news, trying to keep track -
What's happening in France? Has Hitler retreated?
Praying for the time when he would be defeated.

But those poppies, which dance on a summer's day,
Always remind me where our loved ones lay.
Their petals, so intense and splashed with fire
Bring the most precious memories - those which never tire.

Susan Wood

HMS JUNO

*(Sunk off Crete on May 21st 1941
in 2 minutes, with the loss of 116 lives)*

Day after day they waited
for fathers, husbands, lovers and sons
sailing the seven seas to war, bereft of news.

Day after day they sailed braving a barrage of bombs,
tin fish and guns. Loyal men in destroyers, cruisers,
frigates, serving their country.

Day after day they died, anonymous, in fathomless oceans.
Day after day they returned to land marked devastation.

Tears flowed, blood flowed, in swelling streams,
bodies, lives, lay shattered. Future generations denied.
Future generations born. For some survived,
but all had fought insanity, to secure a safe harbour.

Sixty years on, from one dying line,
one line from one letter, stirs the heart to grieve
the unknown. Held where a sea shroud
swirls their steel cold coffin.

No sacrifice should be in vain.
So their descendants must build
on the toughened tissue from invisible scars;

that could make planet Earth
the heritage they died for.

Anita Richards

FLYING BOMBS

Searching blindly through the morning mist
For the flying black cross with its tail on fire,
Fears grip, turn and twist,
Emotions are taut like wire.

De-de-de-de, it throbs away,
The engine relentless and grim.
Will I live to see this day,
Or be blasted limb from limb?

I pray for the engine to go on and on,
For once it stops
And hovers, before spiralling down
All hell drops.

Buildings crumble, glass shatters,
Life is snuffed out in seconds.
Survival alone is all that matters
When stark death beckons.

The bomb passes, I breathe again
Till the next distant sound.
It is enough to drive one insane
And seek shelter deep underground.

Night and day the bombs take aim,
Dust and rubble are all that's left
Of houses, churches, life and fame,
Hope and love, all lies bereft.

To live, breathe and smell fear
Is all consuming, as bombs draw near.
Destruction is at the heart of war,
We should resort to it no more, no more.

S J Dodwell

SUMMER OF 1940

Above green canvas on cheese spread sky
Microdots dart and contact to destroy
A tranquil setting.
Across a static canvas figures freeze . . . watching:
Labourers in crop-laden fields,
Bodies bronzed by heavy summer,
Tense and sigh,
Hoping their dots will conquer
And help preserve 'this blessed plot'
For some future generation.

Evil is rampant:
Valiant young men of knightly stature
Sally forth to slay the dragon;
Below the watchers wait . . .
Praying for victory.

Arthur Pickles

REMEMBER

Remember the good old days and the songs we sang,
Remember the bombs falling, the crashes and the bangs.

Remember the flashes in the cloudy dark sky,
Remember the nights we thought we'd die.

Remember the rations, the queues, the lack of bread,
Remember the tears we shed, as we slept in our beds.

Remember the prayers we spoke, in a bombed out church,
Remember the goat in the yard, and the cockerel on its perch.

Remember the sirens, the blackouts, the Blitz,
Remember the stifling gas masks, that never seemed to fit, *remember*.

Francis Page

NOT AGAIN

When fighting subsided although a relief
We were left with a surplus of tins of corned beef
So it was decreed by the powers that be
It was fine for the feeding of youngsters like me
And mothers must use it, we children must eat
Was it beef with our chips then or chips with corned beef
It would go with potatoes and sometimes with rice
In a sandwich with sauce it was still rather nice
Or she'd dig up an onion to fry in the pan
Disguising the tinned stuff now known as meat flan
Hotted up under gravy it gained a new style
But we did grow to hate it - well after a while
The joy of a rabbit caught out in the fields
Who wasn't quite quick enough showing his heels
Or an egg with some soldiers if you had a hen
You didn't buy boxes of free range back then
But those days are over and I am well grown
And able to choose what I eat on my own
And I'd rather tuck into an old lettuce leaf
Than open another damn tin of corned beef.

Dorothy Blakeman

DOODLEBUG 1944

I heard the two-stroke sounding roar
Reverberating through the sky,
Incoming terror from on high,
That trespassed on the English shore.

And then the gun's cacophony,
All hell let loose, an awful sound,
I dived for safety to the ground,
Still looking up, still keen to see.

I saw it and it seemed a-fire,
Flames streaming from its metal tail,
Immune it seemed to that great hail
Of constant anti-aircraft fire.

But suddenly its engine stopped,
And my heart jumped and missed a beat,
My face turned whiter than a sheet,
I saw it pause before it dropped.

And then it disappeared from sight,
Five seconds, then I heard the bang,
Reverberating echoes rang.
I thought of the poor victims' plight.

Fire engines raced towards the spot
Across the other side of town.
This was the third V1 shot down
In two days - three down on the trot!

Three less of many that got through
To London, but we on the coast
Could thank our gunners, and could boast
We took our share of terror too.

And then I ran for home as fast
As my boy's legs could carry me,
To tell my mum and get my tea,
Relieved that danger was now past.

Jax Burgess

THE RETURN

More than half a century had passed.
Now he was back. He chewed on gum.
Where had the time gone?
He was a man living outside himself.
The memories still flooded back.
He stood alone. What had happened to all the others?
He said a silent prayer and turned away.

Clive Cornwall

LONDON PRIDE

Here's a tribute to those plucky folk
Who defied the London 'Blitz',
And quietly ignored the fact
That they could be blown to bits!
Their courage was amazing,
'Business as usual' they said,
'We may have had a sleepless night,
But at least we're far from dead!'
No one was left without shelter,
As the bombs fell all around,
And even those who lost their homes,
Said, 'Thank God we're safe and sound!'
I'm so proud to be a Londoner
And to have lived those dreadful years
With selfless human beings
Who shared their hopes and fears,
Who supported one another,
Though death rained from above,
And showed in simple actions
That, 'all we need is love'!

Joan Leahy

THE FURIES

The Hawker Furies circled round the school,
All eyes were on them through the narrow panes.
(Our aircraft recognition beat our sums!)
'Sit down! Sit down! Sit down!' yelled Mrs Webb,
The Kestrel engines drowning out her voice
To leave her speechless - something rarely known.
The sounds had faded, one by one they left
The sky a vacuum, void of shapes and sound.
The teacher found she could he heard once more.

The planes had gone - excitement did not die.
They'd landed - so we found by Milton Cross.
The fields around became a tented camp,
Barbed wire reared up to guard the aeroplanes
No, not from Germans, but from white-faced cows
Who longed to lick the fabric from their wings.
In time the airfield grew - control tower - Nissen huts.
A runway stretching to infinity.
The biplanes were replaced by sleeker types
Which schoolboys dreamed of flying, even then.
Some, as they grew, succeeded, died in them.

But all this was to come and much besides,
Evacuees uprooted from their slums,
The blackout, searchlights playing on the clouds
And German bombers droning overhead.
And yet that day - the day the Furies came,
That was the day the war began for me.

David Griffiths

THE WAR . . . THROUGH MY GRANNY'S EYES

I've often sat fascinated, and engrossed,
Listening to my granny relay her childhood tales,
Like the nights spent lying flat out on the beach,
As the air-raid sirens wailed.

Describing how she'd suddenly be woken,
Stunned and startled from her sleep,
As the familiar screeching filled the air,
Warning of the approach of the enemy's airborne fleet.

Adults would be rounding up their families,
In the dark shadows of the night,
All hurrying to fill the sandy shores,
Where they often had to stay till morning light.

They'd lie in unspoken apprehension,
Listening to the bombers fill the pitch-black skies,
Their stomachs knotted, and full of dread,
As tiny children lay sobbing, gulping back their fearful cries.

I'm so glad that she lived through that war,
And her story can be passed down through the generations,
The one thing her reminiscence has taught me,
Is to be sure to pray for peace amongst all nations.

Louise Pamela Webster

ORDINARY HEROES

Up on top of Gran's old wardrobe, by her tea set kept for best
I've come across a battered suitcase, in the spare room kept for guests.
Packed inside are photo albums wrapped up tight against the air,
preserving weddings, births and childhoods, carefully from wear
and tear.
Locked inside, the children voices high-pitched laugh, in faded fields
see them skipping, dance in meadows, gangling limbs and
full cartwheels.

Long before the war was thought of, children innocent of death
climbed up luscious English hillsides, flopping down to catch
their breath;
eyes alight with childish wisdom, summer sunshine in their hair,
playing games of knights in armour, rescuing their ladies fair.

Cameras then were Kodak boxes, 'Must stand still or it will blur!'
Mother pressed the liquorice lever, hear the click and shutter whirr.
Captured in the grainy photos, grinning out in black and white
families of ragged children playing outside day and night.

Here we see them now - all grown up, flapper dresses, shoes
with spats -
gorgeous girls with deep waved tresses, long ago cut off their plaits;
handsome boys in jazzy waistcoats, hair slicked flat with Brylliantine,
arms around shy looking lasses, Edith, Iris, Joan and Jean.

I wonder if they saw war coming, sensed its looming shadows grow
over lives still bright with sunlight? Now I guess we'll never know.
Wait, I see the photos changing - formal portraits, sepia card -
so the war years are beginning: 'Toughen 'em up and train 'em hard.'

Still those grown-up children's faces smiled, 'Just for the
camera please.'
Uniforms for all the young men, WAFS in skirts below their knees.
Smart they looked dressed up - but so young - not yet lost their
friends to war,
hopeful, happy, living, laughing, never had to fight before.

So the children in the suitcase went to war and didn't mind,
most returned from war's destruction, others fate has left behind.
Sealed together in the moment, memories, ancestors past,
times of change, a world of H bombs, won a cold war, peace at last.

Sometimes I hear the children's voices from the suitcase closed
                                                        up tight -
families mixed up together, people's lives in black and white.
Up on top the old oak wardrobe, out of reach but not of mind
now the ones who lived before us live through photos left behind.

I'll end up in the suitcase some day, glossy colour, wedding smile,
'Who's the redhead in the photo?' Then I'll live again awhile.

Joy Lewis

GOT ANY GUM CHUM?

Five was I when war broke out,
Just a little girl,
Living far from the cities,
But I can tell a tale.

Times were hard for our parents,
Dad worked for the SWEB,
Mother cooked and cleaned and sewed,
From morn till we went to bed.

Veg from the garden,
Peas, cabbage and sprouts,
And eggs fresh from the nest,
Rabbit stew and steamed sponge pud,
No one went hungry then.

We amused ourselves by dressing up,
Long frocks and flowers in our hair,
The Yanks came to dances at our village hall,
'Any gum chum?' would fill the air.

Ruby, the girl's rag doll from next door
Played her part in the rescue plan,
When fire drill was being done
She stood nearly as tall as a man.

We had a land girl called Susie,
No strength did Susie lack,
While she polished the floor for my mother,
I rode around on her back!

Oh! Time where have you gone to?
Oh! Folk where are you now?
Oh! Memories are ne'er forgotten.
Oh! I cannot forget somehow.

Rachel Mary Mills

MY MEMORIES OF THE WAR

Yes! I remember the horrors of war!
Whole rows of houses, standing no more.
Landmines on parachutes float silently down
Bringing death and destruction to city and town.

To underground shelters, when sirens we hear,
Bombers approaching! We are warned they are near.
The scream of a bomb, then the target it hits,
All in its pathway is then blown to bits.

The dread of the sight that might meet tired eyes
Of such devastation that rains from the skies.
In these perilous times - how did we cope?
All keeping cheerful - not giving up hope!

Memories grow dim as the years come and go.
Are lessons now learned? Yet it does not seem so!

Greta Gaskin

THAT SUNDAY MORNING

I remember well that Sunday morn in September of '39,
I was helping my mother make cakes and pies and I was aged just nine.
I was weighing currants for cheesecakes - I can see the picture yet,
And we were both singing, happily, in time to the wireless set.
When suddenly, the music stopped and we heard a voice quite sinister,
'We interrupt this programme,' he said, 'to bring you the
                              Prime Minister.'
We both stood still, hardly daring to breathe and I watched as my
                              mother paled.
'The Germans won't listen,' Mr Chamberlain said, 'and negotiations
                              have failed.
And consequently, this country is at war with Germany,' were his
                              final words
And then I saw my mother was crying as her tears fell into the curds.
My grandfather lived two streets away, and didn't have a wireless.
'Go tell your grandad, and run there and back!' And I raced on feet
                              that were tireless.
'There's a war on Grandad, but I mustn't stay, I have to run
                              straight back,
You've to come for your dinner at 5 o'clock if the Germans
                              don't attack.'
As the weeks turned into months our lives began to change . . .
Food was rationed and in short supply . . . many things were strange.
Place names were removed from signposts - you didn't know who
                              was a spy
Streetlights and head-lamps all went out so no one could see from
the sky!
And when you heard the siren wail, to the shelter you must run
And stay there till you heard the 'all clear', it wasn't any fun!
Gas masks were issued, and identity cards, metal railings removed
                              from the garden
And because we lived at the end of the street, my mother was made
                              the street warden.
They brought her a stirrup-pump and 2 pails, marked 'water' and
                              one marked 'sand'.

'Keep these topped up and near the front door, then if a bomb falls
you'll be on hand!
We'll bring you the sand when it's delivered - could be any minute.'
Well the sand never came - it's perhaps just as well cos that bucket
had no bottom in it!
But for the duration of the war it stood behind our settee
Beside the one full of water, and the pump, there for all to see.
My mother never told a soul, believing it's best to keep mum
For if Hitler had known about the bucket he might have dropped
the bomb!

Betty Bee

WAR ON THE HOME FRONT

It's 1944, and I'm 7½, I'm frightened of that nasty Mr Hitler,
And the nasty squander bug, who whispers to housewives to buy,
                                                    buy, buy!
In Dad's shed, there is shrapnel lined up on the shelf, kids' trophies,
Those horrible black-out curtains, and the sounds of Lord Haw Haw
                                        screaming on the wireless,
I'm crying when Tommy Handley died, star of ITMA,
Creeping down to our garden shelter, which we shared with our
                                        bossy neighbours,
Seeing a great big black rat, fat on food from the pig bin, it ran away,
With Mum going down to Bakers' Stores, the manager cutting off
                                        the coupons,
Half of butter, a few eggs, streaky bacon, Mrs Barnes, was all he had
                                        in today.
Dad at his ARP post in Frederick Road, jet-black mackintosh,
                                        rubber boots
Black helmet with a chin-strap, too old for this war, was in the first war,
But Dad still goes up to Piccadilly at the Regent Palace Hotel where
                                        he works,
As a French polisher, seeing the GIs from Rainbow Corner and the
                                        easy-virtue ladies.
I'm going to the pictures with Mum again to see 'The Wicked Lady'
                                        and 'Blood And Sand',
A newsreel came on then seeing thin people dressed in striped pyjamas
                                        in Germany?
I saw the chimneys, I smelt the smell of burning flesh.
My Great Uncle Theodore living in Guernsey, occupied by
                                        the Germans,
'Short commons,' he writes in his Victorian hand, no radios allowed,
                                        but later on,
Sending flimsy white fivers through the post to Dad and Mum and
                                        to the little girl.
Great Uncle was a retired sea captain and had sailed the seven seas.

Thankfully we were all safe, but not so lucky as an HE bomb exploded
in the next street in Frederick Road, killed some families,
leaving number 13 standing, home of my father-in-law to be.
Although I did not know it then, it was all so long ago, and I am 67,
But I remember, us kids had a good war!

Hilda G Hutchin

SOLDIERING ON

Morning, morning, morning,
How could the day begin?
No sight of any sun within me,
The starry skies have gone.

Gone is this basin my home,
Where are those who came before,
The poppies that were once in bloom?
Arid is this forgotten planet,
Inadvertently the wind blows strong.

My last night in this shelter,
Now I must roam once more.
Forever is always forever,
On, the road just calls and calls!

Andrew B Perrins

PREQUEL TO THE THIRD

Be they plentious, poems, of war and despair
Yet still sing we like wanton old song
So little be written of health and repair
'Tis my opinion, that something, is wrong.

That a species discloses its nature
By expression, be written or drawn
If project it the portrait of conflict
Thus unto conflict
New life will be born
For if bloodshed and violence
Shall dwell in our hearts
On our hands, be they certainly worn
Forever discontented
Be the fabric, thus lamented
Of the shroud that so loudly
We proudly adorn

The picture we paint for our children
Should reveal not the acts of such beasts
Let the canvas before them, instil but the image
Of knowledge, and wisdom, and peace

Make we fair sights, that their eyes know no hatred
Grant we fair sounds, for their ears
Teach we them not, of the 'Gunpowder Plot'
Or the war of the 'Hundred Years'
The 'Roses', the 'Civil', the 'Cod', and the 'First'
Are but some of the wars we have heard
Watch ye therefore, for ye'll know not, of worse
If the 'Second'
Is but the prequel
To the 'Third'.

Mark Anthony Noble

SHELTER

Sitting in a shelter bombs droning overhead
keeping up our spirits soon we might be dead
singing all the war songs to block out the noise
children laughing, crying, playing with their toys.
When the war is over and the fear of death has gone
we will have a street party and sing our favourite songs.

Robin Morgan

Unexpected 'Clean Out'

Seaton Viaducts on main London line
Such a target for enemy planes
Flying up high in the moonshine
O'er our country fields and lanes.

The Viaducts, Germans failed to bomb
Though a good many times they tried.
For brave Spitfires with great aplomb
Swiftly chased them far and wide.

To shoot them down 'fore they got away
Was what the Spitfires tried to do,
But p'raps to the bomber pilot's dismay
As fast as him they flew.

Heavy bombs the German aircraft carried.
So, he jettisoned them down to earth.
Neither Spitfires nor the Heinkel tarried,
Flying on for all they were worth.

The Heinkel, he outwitted his foe
And hurried home before it was light.
His load had landed in open fields,
So, no casualties that night.

A farmer who lived near Seaton
Tried very hard to clean out his pond,
But alas, he was always beaten.
(Could have done with a magic wand.)

Next morn, he couldn't believe his eyes,
Saw pond emptied clean as a whistle.
To him this wonderful surprise
Was result of bomber's stray missile!

Loré Föst

A Distant Memory That Never Fades

The gentle rumble begins,
She lifts her face to the sky
Cloaked in clouds the sun not visible.
Is it thunder or a plane?

She raises her face hoping,
Hoping to feel the softness of rain,
On her skin.
She hears the drone of
The air-raid siren.

Her small hand is grasped,
As the crowd floods towards the shelter.
Deeper she swept into the ground.
Absorbed into the belly of the hill.

She strains her ears
To hear a distant crash,
As the protective layer of earth
Shudders and soaks up
Another hulk of steel.

Her upturned face filmed
With particles of soil,
As they float in the air waiting
To scttlc hour aftcr hour.

She closes her eyes
To feel the soft rain
On her skin,
Yet she waits
For the fear of that night
Sixty years ago.

K

THE PEDAL CAR I NEVER HAD THAT WON THE WAR

When I was small it was a time of making do,
of ration books that smelt of bacon, tea and butter
but promised little more than just their smell;
while fathers in proud, nervous ranks went off to war
and mothers darned and spent their days in queues;
when cars and tricycles and metal toys,
forgone for bullets, bombs and submarines,
existed only in a boy's imagination.

Only in dreams was it a time of pedal cars -
and mine was red and sleek and very fast,
kept hidden in the garage in my head,
but real enough for me to hear and feel
each time I filled the garden with its roar
and thrilled crowds with speed records every day.

And, while I dreamed, the pedal car I never had
was dropped with ill-served heroes over Arnhem,
rained terror for terror on Berlin,
slid, silent, under fjords to mine the Tirpitz
and saw the old world end beneath Enola Gay
to make a new one where small brothers could have cars -

by which time I was far too big for one;
and old enough to learn that winning wars
is so much less like winning than it ought to be
to those who hope for dreams.

Martin Parker

FLASHBACK

I stood upon the hill and gazed
as far as I was able;
and saw grey monsters in the sky,
each anchored by a cable.

On the horizon - far away -
a British fleet was sailing.
Dark silhouettes appeared on high
and sirens started wailing.

Next came a droning overhead,
then Spitfires joined the rally;
and searchlight beams cut through the sky,
from way down in the valley.

Bombs whistled down on Brighton town,
the big guns answered back
and tracers streaked across the sky,
to mingle with the flak.

Today I stand upon that hill
and see a dazzling sight,
of vivid lights and screams and bangs,
because it's fireworks night.

Jonathan Bryant

THE REUNION

A brief encounter of the heart - after all those years apart
Was far more than I had ever hoped - our dream had been then to elope

But both our families intervened - dashing hopes as well as schemes
And then you upped and moved away - you were lost . . . as was the day

Now the years they have rolled by - and I still sometimes question why
What the future may have held - If our families they had jelled . . . ?

It just wasn't meant to be - man and wife - yes, you and me
We had married other folk - me a gal and you a bloke . . .

War had come and war had gone - the big bands they still
played our song
Widowed, now I was alone - so were you - quite on your own . . .

Then a friend said, quite by chance - he'd seen in a 'rag' - a local dance
Where old friends go to reminisce - some get drunk - whilst others kiss

And suddenly across the room - came distinctive wafts of your perfume
But I could only stand and stare - For I couldn't see you anywhere . . .

Then as the dancers cleared the floor - I glimpsed a sight of you now
by the door
Time stood still, I called your name - and hoped that you would still
feel the same . . .

Eyes meet and there was still the spark - I take your hand, stroll in the
park
I brush a kiss upon your cheek - it's your heart that I now seek . . .

The day has come we say 'I do!' - you know I'll always cherish you
We've waited such a real long time - now forever you are mine!

Anne E Roberts

My Memory Of World War II

The sad wails of sirens that foretold a noise-filled night;
Gloomy black-out curtains closed, you must not show a light
Windowpanes all patterned with a myriad of paper strips,
And racing to the 'Anderson' for our garden pathway trips.
Maesteg was the venue for 'group six' evacuees.
Though soon back in the Midlands, we were clutching Welsh ID's.
School shelters were spartan and whiffed with oil lamps
But to gain that School Cert, we suffered chills and cramps.
Fireworks on Guy Fawkes, were a dazzling display -
All launched in the lounge, on our high-tech, tin tray!
Shrapnel, searchlights and songs to inspire,
Gas masks, goose grease, a glowing coal fire.
When the final All-Clear sounded, the bells rang out,
With Union flags flying - peace was never in doubt.

Beryl Mapperley

WAR ON THE HOME FRONT

I will always remember the war years,
Though only a young lass of fourteen
I witnessed some scary moments
When the sirens began to scream.

My brother was in the Home Guard,
We were so proud he was guarding us
As we were all propelled to the shelter
Each and everyone in a rush.

I didn't like the gas masks we had to carry every day to school
Yet I felt safe in the shelter under the church
We knew my brother would guard us until the raid was over
And very sure our Lord would never leave us in the lurch.

There were also happy times to remember
When refugees came to stay,
They introduced the wonderful Belgium cakes
And at seventy-eight years of age, I still make them today.

Vera Ewers

Battle O' Britain

I'll speak of the Battle o' Britain
As 'appened not so long ago
When Adolf sought entry to London
And a few lads 'ed to say no

Now Adolf was surely a bad lot
He wanted to conquer ze world
But 'eving bullied his way into Dunkirk
The sea on his jackboots swirled

Not wanting to dampen his moustache
He thought he'd travel by air
It was nobbut ten minutes to Blighty
And he knew where to get a low fare

So he 'ed a quick word with Fat Hermann
Who offered to do him a deal
Despite him being a German
And having a heart made of steel

Fat Hermann said, 'Yes, Mr Hitler
I'm sure I can get you abroad
There's just one or two complications
Some Brylcream Boys likely we'll goad!'

'Fret not about that,' said Adolf
'Have you never met Eva's poodle
It's more fierce than them as spits fire
Besides I have bugs as can doodle.'

Fat Hermann began laying a runway
He found it not much of a trouble
He knocked over one or two houses
Hoping to land on the rubble.

But them as lived near this new airport
Told Hermann to note in his diary
That objecting to t'runway extension
They'd convened a Public Enquiry.

Though Parliament's windows were blacked out
A glimmer of hope through a crack shone
When Winnie addressing the country
Says, 'I want lots of action.'

So t'brave lads of t'spitfire squadrons
With little spare time on their hands
Tells Hermann as Adolf's not welcome
And they'd make sure he nivver lands!

Ower t'white cliffs of Dover they battled
With th'airport contractors and just
Persuaded Fat Hermann to build elsewhere
Before his company went bust.

Said Adolf when told of the outcome,
'Why is it that some folk don't like me?
Nivver mind it's raining in England
So I'll just nip to Russia and ski!'

Steven J Smith

KENT: SEPTEMBER 1940

On the ground the land girls
hoeing, harvesting, backs bent:
tin hats, too hot to work in,
thrown down, protecting only clods of earth.

Overhead, skies blackening,
German bombers droning north west.

The British planes, soaring upwards,
arrowing at the massing shadow,
scattering the darkness,
tracer bullets' staccato shimmer
painting deadly silhouettes.

Those below, running for cover,
hearts and voices cheering,
adrenaline coursing, dodging the debris
- wheels, shards of metal, shell casings -
seeking shelter while spirits rise,
uplifting our lads locked in deadly quadrille.

A spitfire, spiralling to Earth,
bursting in an aureole of flame.
The pilot, silken dome billowing,
drifts in space, returning home.

A shadow, swastika emblazoned,
darts between the paralysed watchers
and the noiseless canopy
weighted with its human pendulum.
A burst of gunfire tears into that silent flight.
The winged image shoots upwards to rejoin the fray.
The parachute floats, lifelessly, down.

Marion Porter

SUMMER 1940
(For Evelyn Hunter)

My one big memory of those pre-school
baby years, is Dunkirk. Not the evacuation,
which I have seen on TV, in the cinema,
heard more reminiscences than I want
or need, but the part my family played
in that drama. Nobody I knew sailed their
cockleshell boat back and forwards
to rescue any of those 338,000 soldiers.

My daddy was away fighting Rommel,
there was no TV to broadcast live
or relay a carefully constructed report;
what I remember, or think I remember,
having heard this piece of family history
so often it has become part of our personal
folklore, is my uncle Duncan's reaction
to trigger-words in the pub or grocer's.

How he staggered straight-armed
and stiff-legged into my Nana's house,
where he was caught and held by Nana
and my other uncle Ramsey, as if bad news
was a net he was endlessly falling into,
gasping out what I thought was his name,
thinking why is he naming himself
over and over, he should know who he is.

I didn't know what 'invalided out' meant,
but later, much later, I realised he was lost
in the enormity of the news about Dunkirk,
unable for that moment to say anything else,
before he launched himself into glass as if
it was water to save or accept him.

Brian Docherty

PLEASE DON'T ASK FOR MORE THAN YOU CAN EAT

One aspect of the war I'll never forget
My empty stomach whilst lying in bed
Itching scabies with scabs galore
My feet bleeding and terribly sore
A whole day walking from farm to farm
Begging for food and trying to charm
I did survive in body and mind
One side effect though . . .
I am not always kind
Especially when seeing food not respected
I then wish for the culprits to be neglected
Of good food and well-being
In stomach and head
Because *binning* large amounts
Is very very bad.

Hans Van Grinsven

TWO DAYS BEFORE D-DAY

Two days before D-Day a young man died,
in an accident, on a road in Kent.

He never saw the littered beaches
or the sacrificed French towns that marked the route to liberation.

He never posed with a captured swastika
for the photographer with his new-fangled contraption.

He never handed his girl, nylon stockings
and her heart's only desire.

Claire Brook

No Flying Tonight

I went to a party in '44, as unique as any can say,
It all took place on a bomber base owned by the USA.
It was New Year's Eve and the WAAF had leave
To accept the invitation.
We were eager to go, though the tramp through deep snow
Somewhat clouded the situation.
Despite wet and cold feet, we wanted to meet
Our neighbours, that side of the forest,
Who with roars and with shake, kept us nightly awake
Taking off in their B17s.
We arrived at the guard post where awaited our host
Who greeted us all with a, 'Hi!'
Then we followed him on with a torch that he shone
On ground cleared of snow and dry.
We got quite a shock when he started to knock
On the door of a big Nissen hut.
I think we'd expected a dance in a hall
And nothing like this envisaged at all.
We were welcomed into a noisy din, by a lively smiling crowd,
But once inside, we stared wide-eyed at the unexpected scene.
There were rows down each side, of orderly beds
Where tired weary boys, daily laid their heads
Returning from nightly Berlin raids.
We met Rod, Speedy, Clint and Buck,
Lewis, Harvey, Carl and Chuck
And other members of their crew.
We looked around to find a chair but saw no sign of any there,
So on the blanketed beds we sat and soon everyone began to chat.
There was so very much to say with these boys far away from the USA,
We danced to their records, we laughed at their jokes,
While they endlessly plied us with popcorn and cokes.
But the time just flew by and midnight came
And orders to be obeyed again.

But as we tramped back on our snow-covered track
One thing was certainly clear -
We knew that we would never forget the crew that we had suddenly met
And now when the planes roared overhead and shook us as
                                        we lay in bed,
There'd be names as we wished them all 'Good luck!'
There'd be Rod, Speedy, Clint and Buck,
Lewis, Harvey, Carl and Chuck,
And we'd pray they would all come safely back.

Irene Locke

REVENGE ON THE DESPOILER

Despoiler of homes, despoiler of lands, despoiler of youth and of men
We are coming to you as avengers. Who will route you out of your den.
We never will cease until we get you, we never will stop in our strides;
We are willing to gain for our children - liberty at expense of our lives.
You called your race the master race - you made of yourself a god,
Inspired your youth with a false hope, ruled them as with an iron rod.
When toys should have been a hobby and games
should have been their fun,
You made of each a soldier and gave to each a gun.
Then you looked for gold, for power and might, you said you
searched for Lebensraum,
But you never heard the widows cry or the child that is left forlorn.
But God's mill is grinding slowly and life's stream is swift and strong
And is dragging you towards the swirling blades of the mill wheel
of the Miller Strong.
The day of reckoning is near at hand. For mercy let you pray,
But this is the gift that is not for you who is done,
You have had your day!

Patrick P McCathy

UNSUNG

Two things defined him,
he was a baker, he was deaf.
He'd just married when war arrived.

Each day his hands were in flour
kneading and shaping to keep people alive.

Each night he dug out bodies
of those who no longer needed his bread,
of those who'd lost so much
they could not taste the taste of life.

He'd cycle home through blitz-dark streets
thinking of the blackness he had seen.

At home was the joy of his new son.
Tomorrow he'd make bread and cakes,
give someone the taste of a smile.

A lorry moved behind him, he couldn't hear.
There were no lights, the driver couldn't see.
Just another casualty of war.

Casual as an ant stepped on by mistake.

They called it manslaughter.
Hero slaughter is what they should have said.

Pam Redmond

20

I am four letters on a slip of white,
And words forced to learn at age to fight,
I have no name, nor sound, but I am written
On scriptures by soldiers and mothers of Britain,
Who I have never seen,
And those who will no longer be,
What I was then -
A soldier of twenty.

I am voiceless, silent, like all the rest,
Sorley's mouthless and Brooke's English best.

They all learn my story,
Learn it off by heart
And reel it off to show how smart
They each can be.
But they don't care about them or me.

Four letters on a slip of white,
The nameless etched, engrained in their head.
Voiceless, lost and forced to fight.
We are one word.
We are the dead.

Lianne Lee

WAR ON THE HOME FRONT

Up our way we didn't see much of the war
and the aircraft that flew by
were ours and went unhindered
in a clear and friendly sky.
They'd test the sirens weekly,
we'd hear guns on the local range
but the war that we saw on the newsreels
seemed so far away, so strange.
Then one night our peace was shattered
by the siren's warning wail
and I'll never forget how my mother's face
in an instant had turned pale.
We heard the uneven engine beat
and then a chilling sound,
the crump, the thump, the heart-sickening bump
of bombs as they struck the ground.
What seemed like an eternity passed
till the sirens called 'all-clear'
and mole-like from the ground we crept
to the bitter first taste of fear.
We later learned a damaged plane
had jettisoned bombs - and more
as it tried to head across the sea
to a far less hostile shore.
We were fortunate living through a war
that remained a far-off fight
but I still remember to this very day
how I grew up that night.

Donald S Ferguson

ALIVE IN FORTY-FIVE

Helter-skelter to the shelter
At the sound of the siren's wail
With broken sleep, that made us weep
Wondering when peace would prevail
My sister, mother and brother
One bunk and a little armchair
Mother prayed in her gentle way
She believed, God was with us in there.
Our heat and light came through the night
From a littler battered oil lamp,
In blankets wrapped, sometimes we napped
For our refuge was cold and damp.
Songs we'd sing and Mother would bring
Laughter, funny stories galore!
Widowed in her prime, at a bad time
We children, were all she lived for.
Through the years of laughter and tears
Many nocturnal trips were made
Though life was tough as we grew up
Foundation of love, Mother laid.
At last came peace and happy release
In nineteen forty-five.
We prayed and cried for those who died
And thanked God, we were still alive.

Patricia Whittle

A Memory Of 41/42

I hear the 'planes fly overhead as I lie nightly in my bed
I know from engine sounds they make and by direction that they take
whether they are friend or foe, as on their deadly way they go
Perhaps they've been across the sea, blasting others, such as we
and are now returning home, tired and weary, having flown
for hours from some forsaken place, where once were buildings
now just space
If they're foe and visiting us, carrying fire and noise, and just
the other day I heard the sound of bombs, without regard
dropped on people, kids and all in Belswain's Lane, quite
near the school
But this an isolated case, dropped in error or in haste
No target here that I can see
Just a railway and a factory.
In daylight too the other day, I saw a 'dogfight' in the sky
this was in the afternoon, one day in the middle of June
Dornia bombers flying high and Spitfires trying to destroy
The cannon-fire was loud and clear and the scream of engines
seemed quite near as I watched in awe, neck strained back
as the Spitfires mounted their attack
I was out delivering bread that day, in Deaconsfield Road,
I have to say
And taking loaves to Mrs Floyd, knocking her door, which
was open wide, no one came but a voice replied from the garden
'Want to come inside? Take cover in the shelter here until the siren
sounds 'all-clear'?
'No thanks,' I said, 'I must push on, lots to do and they'll soon be gone,
scrapping there up in the sky.' Moving all the time away,
away from sight and soon from sound
as though they'd never been around.

John Gilbert Slade

SOME OF MY MEMORIES OF WORLD WAR II 1939 - 1945

I was nearly seven years of age when World War II broke out
I was too young to understand what it was all about
As time went on my parents had to take in evacuees
These children were missing their families they were a
                              bit out of control and did as they pleased
My mother had a difficult time with them but with her
                                        gentle loving care
She would put her arms round these children and treat them very fair.

Clothing coupons were introduced in 1941
60 coupons each which had to last 15 months for everyone
There were slogans advertised for all to make do and mend
I would often be passed hand-me-down clothes that
                              belonged to my mother's friends
My aunt gave me a bathing costume made of wool
It was a perfect fit until I got into the swimming pool.

The utility scheme was introduced in 1942.
It was designed to save materials, for me and you
With fewer buttonholes and less pleats.
The children's clothes were cheaper and they didn't get so crushed,
                              when we sat down on our seats.
Ladies', gents' and children's hats were coupon-free, that was a treat.
It made people look and feel smart when they walked down the street.

As food became scarcer, on the 29th September 1939,
Identity cards and ration books, were issued for everyone down the line
The official day of food rationing known as 'Coupon Monday' was
                              the 8th January 1940; that was very good
The government was doing a great job, and was making sure that
                              everyone was getting their fair share of food.

People had to have black curtains or shutters on their windows at night
ARP wardens would check houses when it got dark to see that there
                              wasn't even a chink of light
When there was an air raid the sirens would be so loud and
                              go off with a belter
We didn't always get time to go to the air raid shelter

My parents would get us all together and we would go under the stair
My father would have us down on our little knees
And he would be deep in prayer.

One Sunday evening, my family and I were all travelling over
The Kincardine Bridge,
which could be opened up to let large ships through.
When the sirens went my father knew what he had to do
He had to be slick and get off that bridge, quick!

This is a few of the things that took place that I can
                                    remember of during the war years.
Which brought sadness and joy, also laughter and tears,
That have seen our family through sixty long years.

Rosina Forward

CHILDHOOD MEMORIES

I remember waking in the middle of the night
to the sound of a noise that filled me with fright.
The air raid sirens were going once more
as people awoke and headed for the door.
To the back street shelters we all would go,
who would return? We did not know.
As the Germans dropped their bombs of hate
inside the shelters we would sit and wait.
As the enemy planes flew over on their flight
the shipyard was the place in their sight.
Most of the bombs were dropped in haste
but many buildings were put to waste.
Then the all-clear sirens would wail once more
and our town became the same as before.
It's over sixty years now but I will never forget
the sound of those sirens which haunt me yet.

Robert Beach

BLASTED IN MID-AIR

The tangled up molten metal mash
Pulp of cremated and trash
The 3-D flattened Panzer tanks!
No sweat, get it off your chest
The truth drug can it be
You see and flee
So now it's like wise - see!
Were grass once again so green
The ashes cast a shadow
Mine still on a spectre of light
And like inspectors, we ditch them
Hooray, the National Anthem.
The mouldy bread on the stove
Back in Lime Grove
Shattered at their missing home
And goodness on the morrow
Kiss away the sorrow
For there's plenty of grub
We all dug up the greens
And came back with a full wheelbarrow
The animals fell 'para'
The paratroopers in Parka's
Would carry on by markers
And blast away using mortars
An arm or a leg you'd be crackers
But I've give you this son
You sure made me proud!

Hardeep Singh-Leader

War On The Home Front

Living in fear of the unknown was paramount for all,
Changes in day to day living soon became the norm.
Three years as a civilian was only one side of the coin
Faced with wartime changes was preparing me to join.

Never could the toss of a coin by considered for this,
When wheels are set in motion, they do not miss,
A vital call-up to serve the country and each other,
Giving a training, second to none with our sisters and brothers.

Keeping the home fires burning meant paying the price,
Queuing for food and huddled together in air raid shelters most nights
Issued with ration books, clothing coupons and gloomy unlit
                                                    street lights
Gas masks in brown boxes, carried everywhere by day and by night.

The eerie wail of sirens sent a chill throughout the family,
The heavy drone of bomb laden planes, sent us below ground for safety,
Husbands, sons, brothers and sisters called to serve on land,
                                                    sea or Air Forces,
Woman and girls into the land army, on the buses and as munitions
                                                    factory workers.

I reassured myself, wasn't I in the war already?
I then learned there were many girls like me who dreaded the process
of being transformed into a soldier,
Fearfully brave when leaving home and trying to be bolder.

My army number W/215449. I automatically remember,
With true friendships for life, by strangers brought together,
And in that setting I met the man I wed,
To share new hope for our future on the paths we tread.

God's peace and love are our innermost needs,
Self discipline is necessary now we are free,
Discipline with love for children in the home,
And compassion for others who do not know.

These lessons in life are simple but true,
Until we take more care of each other, wars will rule.
God made people, black, brown, yellow and white from the same mould
To trust Him means nothing can separate us from His loving hold.

Kathleen McBurney

NEAR THE HOME FRONT

Increasingly the sky, thundering, seems high and strong,
Seeming almost dangerous even during the quiet moments
Lightning flashes over the saltmarsh and the long high moments
                                        of danger
After that the quiet and the water runs down the hill in rivulets
And down the sides of the homes . . . in the quiet of the homes.

Michael C Soper

PARADOX

They often say, 'In the good old days.'
The days that have gone, no longer replayed.
'Remember!' they say, 'when food was on ration?
We all pulled together, as one, this nation.'
So they shared what they could spare,
All united in the country's despair.
A sense of worth, a sense of pride,
Existed for all with no class divide.
It's all so sad, wouldn't you agree?
That only devastation brings this unity.

Sara Church

LAST LINE OF DEFENCE

Cwm Garw had no strategic worth,
A land-locked cleft with cruel slope
Its value lay deep in the Earth
That brave men mined for victory and hope.

No signs or spies nor anti-aircraft gun,
No docks or dams nor ball-bearing shed
No military might to attract the Hun,
No siren call to shake us from our bed.

Black-out yes! Queues and rationing, yes!
But no famine here or nutritional stress
From over-counter, under-counter or the garden plot
All but the exotic came and went, no one cared a jot.

We saw and heard 'planes Cardiff bound
Also to the west, resistant Swansea Town,
And despite 'The Arsenal' pilots could not see
Cwm Garw was safe haven for the child evacuee.

Deep mines decreed that most men must remain
But no white feathers here as volunteers left
To serve a king and country, oblivious of the pain.
The telegrams arrived on time and families were bereft.

The Home Guard preened and marched and drilled,
Staged a battle, real guns that fired blanks.
Young boys got in the way of grown-up pranks,
Friend and foe entrained to pub, no one ever killed.

Sunday morning after church, excitement grew,
The firemen drained the river in their bid
To douse pretending flames and train the crew
Of butchers and bakers whose skills were barely hid.

No bombs, doodle-bugs or rockets inward bound
Spoiled our way of life but we partied with rest
On May the eighth and after, believing Britain still was best.

Mike Hayes

BLITZ MEMORIES

There it goes again! The air raid warning.
German bombers are heading our way.
Our night will be spent until the morning
Taking refuge from the birds of prey.

The Anderson shelter is our lair for the night.
Like a large iron dog kennel, half buried in the soil,
It could not be called a pretty sight
But its construction cost many hours of toil.

With fork and spade until we were whacked,
In the back lawn we dug a large pit.
Then we assembled the shelter and packed
The earth dug out to cover it.

Not always is the siren our first alert
To abandon the house for the lawn.
We have learned to take to the dirt
When other events do us warn.

There could be searchlights showing their glare
Or our own guns blasting the atmosphere.
Or BBC radio going off the air
To deny the enemy a course to steer.

The most urgent warning has a unique tone
Which experience has taught us to sense.
It's the Luftwaffe's engines' rhythmic drone,
A noise to make us feel tense.

Our own planes have an unmodulated whine,
A sound our ears love to track.
For to us it is a comforting sign
That we are hitting them back.

Bert Maskell

THE BOMBARDIER'S BOOTS

Of all the tortures for new recruits
There's none so grim as their rock-hard boots,
Their struggles with them will never cease -
All spit and polish and elbow-grease.

When buffed and burnished their toe-caps shine
As the Colonel inspects the eager line,
They march and wheel on the barrack square
And one Bombardier is the smartest there.

He grows in stature, a soldier born
He drills and trains from dust to dawn
To go to war in a foreign land -
All pride and glory and 'Follow the Band!'

But his platoon is badly deployed,
Nineteen years old and his dreams destroyed,
The raid is doomed as the Germans thrust
He has no choice, surrender he must.

Herded in seemingly endless files
Force-marched for over 500 miles
His boots are now worth their weight in gold
As he tramps through mud and rain and cold.

Time marches too, sixty years and more;
Emotions subside, no longer so raw
But thrown on a tip, one tattered boot
Recalled the boy who marched that route.

Lorna Carleton

THE SNIPER

The soldier aimed and fire the shot,
Out flew the bullet, straight and hot.
It reached the target in the chest,
Ripped apart the bone and flesh.
The pain, it was too much to take,
With God he had his peace to make.
The man fell slowly to the ground,
Now still and silent, not a sound.
The soldier watched then moved away,
He had now earned his bloody pay . . .

Tony Morgan

DICTATED PEACE

President and Prime Minister's kids
Gonna screw up the world, just like they did.
Generations down the line, things are gonna be the same,
Can't do no complaining, we all gotta take the blame.
F**k society! F**k ever living in a democracy!
Dictated and capitalist is all this world is ever gonna be.
Two world wars, no peace ever gonna be achieved.
'A peace for our time,' the f*****s actually believed.
Butcher, maim, fight and kill,
Learn from our mistakes, screw that, we never will.
Justify your wars; lie to the entire community,
Sell this world's peace you f*****s, but don't try and indoctrinate me.

Sarah Sproston

THE DARK SOUL OF MAN

Creeping out of his subconscious
like ooze from a corpse,
the dark soul of Man
slithers forward
one putrefield limb
at a time.

Intolerance, indifference,
misplaced jingoism spawns,
terrorism, rape, murder . . .
War
the abhorrent play
of the Devil's dedicated disciples.

Having perverted the message of his Gods,
Man rejoices in his lust for blood,
a faithful attendant to his ungodly master.
Hidden within the shroud of
truth and justice thrives
the dark soul of Man.

Polly Davies

THE BRAVE

I walk the leafy lanes I know so well,
Lost in the gentle stirrings of a peaceful vale.
Of gratitude for this, I have no better tale,
Than the one the silent stones can tell.
Their names flood the land they fought to save,
In church, on hill, on roadside cross,
I count them all as one, the brave,
Who for my freedom paid the cost.
I never heard the sirens sound,
The whistling skies, the engines drone
I never huddled underground,
Or saw the fires take my home.
I never knew such desperation
The wrench of loved ones leaving;
Of loss with such bitter consolation -
A nation bound in grieving.
I never crossed the fields of rank despair
And saw the thousands fall,
Or battled in the putrid air,
In answer to the call.
Their names flood the land they fought to save,
In church, on hill, on roadside cross,
I count them all as one, the brave,
Who for my freedom paid the cost.

Jan Marshall

YESTERDAY?

As silence falls upon the scene
Did something happen - or was it a dream?
As birds fly on high, singing their song
Did something yesterday then somehow go on?
As the tide did ebb and so retreat
Did I hear the sound of marching feet?
Did many gather to greet a dawn
Was a new day yesterday - perhaps then born?
Did thousands attend to convey respect -
Did friends of old get the chance then to connect?
On sea in ship - or in air above
To rejoin lost ones who they still love
Those who then braved and opposed our foes
Beyond the shore against which water flows
High up on hill or in vale below
Where lay the lost ones that once they did know
Of our own isle and from lands far beyond
The closest of kin of whom we were most fond
Who fought for peace on a distant shore
Who have now gone, now and ever more
A silence still does reign in a manner supreme
But I do now know that it was not a dream
Yesterday meant much to both you and me
For on that day they landed in Normandy
In bunker in trench, whichever then sought
To free the French our fighters then fought
Yes something did happen - though sad -hooray!
That day of destiny we now know as D-Day.

Jon El Wright

A Country Hard At War

It destroys like a cancer
It lies open like a sore
Hear the sound of marching feet,
A country hard at war

In the name of religion,
More important than the poor
Machine guns at the ready,
It's the mighty sound of war

In the name of freedom
For the sake of common law
The suicide bomber is waiting
At the door

The bombs are falling all around
The destruction and the gore
You can almost smell the fear
Of a country hard at war

Grace Divine

GREAT BRITAIN AND THE UNION JACK

So proud were we as children of Britain and her flag,
We weren't afraid to speak our mind. We even used to brag.

On Empire Day we'd proudly boast the Union Jack's renown
The only thing we mustn't do was draw it upside down.

To be a British citizen was honourable and true
To serve the king and country was what we aimed to do.

Where is that pride that we did boast, to shout out clear and loud
To salute our very heritage of which we were so proud?

Where are the values we portrayed and honoured every day
With homage to our place of birth and unafraid to say?

The glory of old England's flag still flies, though pride has passed,
A-withered in the winds of time and drooping on its mast.

Helen E Utting

WAR AND PEACE

Humanity cries out for peace
Generations weep through each war
yet hatred, poison, jealousy
permeate people devastatingly.
Religions and politics play their part
frequently misconstruing so much.
Oh how power and arrogance damages,
seeing the millions of innocent suffer
in this 21st century,
who can honestly define terrorism?
The global need is for understanding,
honest communication and decency
all expressed without religion politics
or power games,
then a true sense of caring
can be recognised for the common good.
Listen for peace each and every day.

Margaret Ann Wheatley

MEMORIES OF D-DAY

I was in the D-Day landings
but not in the leading wave
And when stepping onto Normandy beach
saw many new-dug British graves

The artillery of the German force
was still playing its deathly song
That crossing the beach and through this hell
the soldiers' nerves had to be strong

You heard the shouts from wounded men
needing stretcher bearers' attention
But some had died before they came
their deaths were past prevention

There were many acts of bravery
upon this war-torn beach
From men who followed Jesus Christ
with the heights they tried to reach

The comradeship amongst the soldiers
was a beautiful thing to see
That I knew whilst standing on the beach
this was the end of tyranny

Lachlan Taylor

11.11.11

When I broach the gates of Heaven
I shall ask to meet one man.
He'll be a British general -
I will find him if I can,
for I wish to ask him quietly
by what vicious logic he
decided World War One should end
so punctiliously.

'Bar steward! Look sharp with the good old XO!
Advance Madame Cognac!
Now, chaps, here's a go!
The game's damn near run! We've trounced Willi Hun!
So, let's set the our for the call, Battle's done!
Tomorrow prior lunch. What?
Say, well before one.'

While we recognise the quaintness
of this famed Eleventh Hour
on the Eleventh Day no less
of this final month of pow'r,
I must ask him if he gave a thought
for a Tommy in the line
who, looking out across the wire,
died at ten fifty-nine.

Waterman Quill

THE PRICE OF FREEDOM
(Written after coalition troops were hit by friendly fire killing civilians, soldiers and injuring many)

Hands tied and hooded - they sit in the sand
Terrified prisoners in their war-torn land
Saddam's image torn from its base
God preserve our human race
Help our troops to free their land
No more blood in the desert sand
Now a missile's been fired from an American plane
Bombed our own troops - such pain, such pain
Troops and reporters injured and killed
The price of freedom on which we build
Comfort the families of those we mourn
Look forward to a peace reborn
Support our troops in this troubled time
All the world will know a peace sublime
God give them courage to fight the fight
To strive for peace we know is right.
Show compassion, kindness, love
Then peace not missiles from above

Maryska Carson

MY GARDEN OF MEMORIES

In my garden of memories I'll grow bright poppies red,
The colour of the blood that on a foreign field you shed.
Fragrant rosemary I'll plant in remembrance of you,
And sweet forget-me-nots with flowers of misty blue.
Crimson roses will bloom beneath the blue, summer sky,
To show that my love for you will never die.
The heady, evocative scent of chrysanthemums will fill the
autumn of my years,
And I'll remember our spring, when the daffodils danced, and
smile at the memory through my tears.

Anita Cooling

RELIGIOUS TOLERANCE?
(Sonnet to a Street Evangelist)

Sure? Mere mortal man, pray, why is it so
That you are right, and have yourself no doubt,
That of the gods their numbers all you know?
And one to you has given that right to shout
Out loud to those who pass you by - sincere,
As you, believing other versions of the truth,
If truth has place in all religion's sphere,
For none, of truth, can furnish any proof.

Whose god is it who blesses on each side
Those soon to kill the other for his cause?
Does hate, not love, deep in religion hide,
To fester all mankind with needless wars?
Can ever peace, midst faiths' created hells,
Stem needless tolls on life, and

death's dull funeral bells?

Douglas Bryan Kennett

A VISION OF DEATH AND HORROR

The arms of the US are waiting to pounce
Saddam Hussain, Bush wishes to trounce,
Soldiers from Britain and Australia could be there too
Which would be a foolhardy thing to do.
A massive force is surrounding Iraq
Waiting for the order to attack,
When that time arrives, whether night or day
The forces of the west may not have their own way.
In the desert no Iraqi tank can be found
Saddam's army has gone underground,
To fight in close combat in the streets of Baghdad
Where the wounded and death toll may be very bad.
I see in my vision of death and horror
Innocent men, women and children seeing no tomorrow,
US and British solders may meet their match
In the streets of a city which is not their patch.
Civilian men, women and children may take up the gun
To avenge the loss of a daughter or son,
Soldiers of the west may die in this hell
Nothing may be gained, perhaps an oil well.
Bush what will you unleash, who can tell?
You may release forever the demons of Hell,
So think again before the final shot
Before the stench of death and bodies rot.

David G Forsbrook

WAR AND PEACE

Weapons, wounds, war, wounded, why
Artillery, ammunition, armour,
Rifles, radios, ropes, reasons.

Armies, air force, aid,
Nations, navy, nurses,
Death, dangerous, distraction, doctors, destruction.

Peace, prisoners, paramedics, paras, prison, people,
Everlasting, encouragement, escape,
Aeroplanes, annihilation,
Courage, choppers,
Execute, extermination.

Michelle Knight

THE TWIN SISTER

Many a night
I stood before the altar
And saw her face in the twilight
Of the window; and saw the rainbow.
I had been in uniform
And sometime before
The dreaded thunder of the guns
Had brought me to my knees,
Haunted my ears;
The black ravens had flown overhead
And the skulls and bones lain all around
As I heard their calls, saw each corpse,
Saw each coffin before the altar;
Each had escaped, many procured bodies
From cemeteries and presented them to the authorities
As theirs anonymously,
And taken on false names,
Gone on their merry ways, and
Lived their lives
After the bodies had been identified
As their own
By transferring their characteristic chromosome;
'Hallucinations . . .' whispered the enquiry,
'Victims of insanity . . .'
But, I had seen her, in the trench,
Her spirit,
And that is why I had escaped
From the asylum
And
Lived with my twin sister.

David de Pinna

NATIONS AT WAR

The footsteps of man tread hard and deep.
In the war-torn ruins and trenches so deep,
The bodies of soldiers piled high in a heap,
The cost of war is much, only lives are cheap.

Over the top the cry goes out
Men and boys too afraid to shout,
Shells explode flames soar high,
This band of men blown into the sky

When will it end? No one can say,
Perhaps when there are no more lives to pay.
These families are parted thoughts are of home
Reality comes back quickly when others
Are heard to moan,
This is wanton murder.
Please, please God, send me home.

Lennard Clarke

SOLDIER BLUE

He stands alone
this brave defender,
a child of yesterday,
unsuspecting of the danger
that fate will bring his way.

He finds a smile
this action man,
dressed for the occasion,
home suddenly invades his thoughts,
then fades with some persuasion.

Oblivious to disaster
impending by the hour,
he battles through the day,
with innocence his loved ones
for his safe return all pray.

Now he must lie
where before he stood -
a mother's precious son,
the life that was waiting to happen
left draining by the gun.

Janice Mitchell

THE TURNING POINT

People paused, that long-forgotten glorious sound to hear,
The sound of lofty steeple bells, stilled for many a year.
Now they chimed across the land, ringing loud and long,
Pealing out with ecstasy their sonorescent song.
Ringers, summoned hastily, tolled their dusty ropes,
And booming belfries everywhere inspired the nation's hopes.
The very air was filled with noise, rumbling like thunder,
And people stood, amid the sound, gazing up in wonder.

Somebody came forward who was eager to explain,
'Our troops have won a victory out there at Alamein.'
Was this to be the turning point? Churchill had no doubt,
Triumphantly he spread the word, 'Let the bells ring out.'
And so they rang throughout that day as never rang before,
To celebrate the victory that turned the tide of war.
Despite the hardships still ahead, and great the price to pay,
Hearts and minds were lifted high on that November day.

Frank Jensen

BRITISH HEROES

They fought in the world's darkest days
Their vision was plain to see
Of people going their separate ways
In lands that were totally free

They fought through a living hell
They knew they had to win
Many buried where they fell
So a better life could begin

They left their families safe at home
And sailed they knew not where
The coming battle must be won
To lose they did not dare

For freedom they gave their lives
The greatest sacrifice ever made by man
The government of today doesn't give a damn
They'll hand it all to Europe with not a single care

Will the modern spineless British led by Tony Blair
Seal the fate of Britain?
Euros or our heroes did they die in vain
In their countless thousands our freedom to retain?

Euros or our heroes where does Britain want to be
Under the yoke of Europe or keep our sovereignty?
Our soldiers, sailors, airmen died so we'd be free
So keep the pound you know, it's sound the price of liberty.

B D Vissian

THE SOLDIER

The soldier sitting on the front line, in the trench he looks fine.
What's going on in his head, awaiting the signal to attack ahead?
Sheer terror and disbelief, adding to the people's grief
The bell rings out, off we go, over the top, into the unknown.
Running behind is his best friend, he drops to the floor, is this the end?

Adrenaline pumping, people shout, 'Is this the final one? Please
                                                    get me out.'
Sheer panic all around, dying bodies on the ground.
Please let this be a nightmare, don't let it be true!
Howls out to his young ones, 'I want to be with you,'

Shells and bullets flying past, clouds of dust fill his mask,
The dead bodies on the ground we pass.
Where will it lead? I don't know what lies ahead of this dreadful show.
One to one, he's in conflict, if he kills him, he'll be sick.
'Shoot before he shoots you,' a voice rings out, in his head, it's true.
It's not an easy thing to do, he can see his eyes, they look
                                                    straight through.

Two shots ring out from his rifle, on the ground the enemy falls,
As he runs, he gets a hot, sharp pain in his leg. Now he is lame.
'Is this the end for me? I can't go back until we are free.'
His head spinning, his body numb, 'I'm afraid, please help me, Mum!'
When he wakes he's back at base, he will be taken home with haste.
What is the point of war? It ruins our lives and kills rapport.

Marilyn Pullan

For King And Conscience

Onwards Christian soldiers, and we marched off as to war,
with the cross-hairs of the sniper, going on just as before.
If the Devil took the high most, then pray who went to Heaven?
I had many a friend at seven o'clock, not many were left at eleven.
But by Jove what a sight, what a sight at very first light,
Blighty would always go forward and fight,
and then we knew all about war and fright.
And for those who objected their prospects were black,
- for cowards were branded with a bullet in the back.
Dulce et Decorum Est.
- an old, old lie, but simply the best.
They cheered us off to a six-week war,
my papers were stained with so many more.
Four years it was . . . it seemed like a score.
I cracked my whip on a stiff upper lip, so stiff it never spoke,
the fun all fled when we got to the front, and he never saw the joke.
Screams of the men must not be heard, their rank not filed in our minds,
but when Eton and the East End bleed together, it's a sign of
                                            dying times.
Dirty work, time for a drink, and what's the toast to be?
Oh to be home and having tea, with a sweetheart whom I'll never see,
for this hungry shrapnel feeds all around,
and the Hun so horribly fights for the ground,
they weren't for running . . . that much we found.
Here lies Jack, for his gallantry stacked, his union of life repealed,
he bravely went and did his bit, but bought some cold, hard steel.
So the next time you salute the dead, be sure to tell your sons,
for war is wretched, take my word, and soldiers die so young.

Sean Kinsella

REMEMBRANCE - A SOLDIER'S STORY

(Dedicated to the servicemen/women past and present who gave their all for our precious freedom)

That's it now, it's all over,
The battles fought and won,
So many strong brave young men,
Looking down the barrel of a gun.
At home their loved ones waiting,
In anxious nervous fear,
The dreaded arrival of a telegram,
A most painful shed of tears.
Now a new tomorrow is dawning,
A vessel carrying casualties arrives,
The relief of being back on home ground,
Though so many lost their lives.
A soldier's war is not over,
For it's only just begun,
The haunting painful memories,
Of battles he's fought when young.
Remembrance is a time to reflect,
Each soldier a story to tell,
Remembrance to hold a memory of the brave
Young men that fell.
Alone in peaceful silence,
A cenotaph surrounded by men,
All bearing a red poppy,
Reliving their war again.
'It's all in the past,' the young may say,
They know not of war and fear,
'Tis for this very reason we owe,
The young of yesteryear.
For our soldiers we should all remember,
Bearing medals proudly standing in line,
Who sacrificed their precious lives,
That we may know peace in our time.

Michele Simone Fudge

RUSTY CHAINS OF THE DEEP CHIME

Rusty chains of the deep chime,
In unison their death rhyme,
Men lost in deep, deep sleep.
In the vesseled ruins in oceans keep.
Seaweed tangles, they lie rock bottom,
Forgotten graves in oceans deep.

Deep in sandy ruins buried bones,
Of men who never returned home,
The bell tolls for lost souls,
Watery graves of the long forgotten,
Rusty chains of the deep chime,
In unison their death rhyme.

Rachel Lucinda Burns

GRANDAD'S WAR

'Were you in the war, Grandad, and if so, which one?'
'Yes, I was in the Great War, Grandson, and oh, it we won!'
'What was great about it, Grandad, was it loads of fun?'
'No it was loads of blood and gore, and me with a tommy gun!'
'Then how come you call it great, Grandad? Sounds no fun at all.'
'Ah but me and all me mates were there, and we stood very tall!'
'So do you have reunions, Grandad, to see them all again?'
'Only in my nightmares, Grandson, and there they will remain!'

A Dyas

WAR REQUIEM

This solace of being
The mind fixed on meditation
This war requiem to the dead.
For this sea becomes part
Of a Suffolk landscape
Religion around these built walls -
That harbours a soul's calling -
The first rehearsal
Light-headed I watch
Those incoming waves
And turning tides
That inner light
Of instruction -
To one solitary gull
Who rides the waves -
And the incoming fishermen
To light the mind
From danger -
And put Christ in their hands
And face storms
And her cries.

Roger Thornton

THE COLOUR OF SPRING

We do not die with the red autumn leaves
Nor on the white plains of winter, like birds
We die in spring, beneath the budding trees
Oh yes, it was a funeral march you heard.
We die as white lilies of the valley
As bright and blue-eyed as forget-me-nots
We die in the arms of a green lady
The world turning grey as the cuckoo mocks.
We die in the warmth and beauty of spring
In scented hyacinths and sweet blossom
We die in black birdsong, as church bells ring
In a red river of blood of the lamb.
How many colours of spring will be lost
For an empty cave and a broken cross?

Susan Wren

POCKETBOOK

Amid the armouries
shell-shocked soldiers
bawled bravely, like babies
the bravado wearing thin on top
like my uniform where I kept
the love letters which wept
their longing tears of miles
but smiles at the bravery
the medals they pinned to me
but if I died the thing
I was most afraid they'd see
was my book
of sketches of places and parts of faces
blown off. Some of friends.
Of the stories I wrote when I
thought I may die
alone in a field
where I didn't mind if
they find my limbs
or nothing of me
as long as I could hide
inside what I felt
in my pocketbook
I allowed my soul to melt.

Audrey Marshall

A Plea For Peace

I read in the papers, every other day,
    That another soldier, has lost his life,
Leaving behind, little children,
    And also, a very young wife.

Because, it seems, as one war ends,
    Another one will start,
With some country invading another's land,
    Or ruled by a dictator, without a heart.

So wouldn't it be wonderful,
    If leaders, of all countries, could agree
To all shake hands and be good friends,
    And make the world's people, feel free.

Jean Hendrie

THE EVIL OF WAR

When the silver bugle sounds
For the soldier to jump from his bed,
It isn't death's sting he simply dreads,
It is the agonising thoughts of
Mutilation.

Eileen Barker

I HAVE A DREAM

Although in my seventies, I still have a dream
that war is no more and peace reigns supreme,
that men with their power will see common sense,
use passion, compassion, not sit on their fence.
That cruelty and envy will no longer bring tears
and the sound of men marching will no longer cause fears.
But we ordinary people have more than one dream,
forever embracing our families so dear.
Could not the world's rulers have respect for life's scheme,
and banish their pride, bring pity to bear?

June Picken

A DIFFERENT KIND OF FRONT LINE

People imprisoned without charge,
Tortured, mocked, then jeered.
Was this why we fought a war,
To become a nation to be feared?
Weapons of mass destruction
Still haven't yet been found,
Though lots of innocent bodies
Are lying dead upon the ground.

All the dead belong to someone,
No wonder people are distraught.
Watching this endless slaughter
Wasn't the outcome we sought.
Suicide bombers, from Al Qaeda
Make it much harder to understand
How we can begin to deliver peace
To that war-torn, troubled land.

Send the soldiers home, people say,
Let the Iraqis sort themselves out.
But we created all their problems,
So we must do more than shout.
We didn't expect to wage a war
On hundreds of innocent civilians,
Back home people marched in protest
But politicians ignored the millions.

We were told we were on a mission
To set all the oppressed people free,
But we've become an occupying force
And that doesn't seem right to me.
All peoples must strive for peace
So this oil grabbing war can cease.

Mavis Simpson

THE TRAVESTY THAT IS WAR

We're living in a tragic world where evil seems to reign,
And hearts are overflowing bitter tears from all this pain.
Whenever will it end, I hear your devastated cry,
So many lives are lost; and we are left to question why.

It seems so mindless; almost like a riddle, meaningless,
We're sinking even faster in the depths of this abyss.
There has to be much more to life, where's God in all of this?
Bewildered we cry out; it echoes, hollow in the mist.

God's heart is breaking as He looks; society's so flawed,
He made us and He bought us, He so longs to be adored.
But free will gave us too much choice and we have turned aside;
Regretfully we often fail to let Him be the guide.

While widows weep and mothers mourn the loss of loved ones slain,
The sound of weaponry drones on across the arid plain,
Why doesn't god take action now, reverse this obscene loss?
And yet He asks no more than He faced on that cruel cross.

He uses pain for deepening our sensitivity
To life by making characters as strong as they can be.
Our image will be like His own; He died to set us free,
And by His power we'll turn things round, so every eye will see.

Pain, accidents, death tragedy will raise the question why,
It causes personal anguish, why did that Korean die?
Emotions running high, and anger at this pointless loss,
We love the sinner, hate the sin, like Jesus on the cross!

So Lord please help us make some sense of misery and pain,
We know You died and rose again for our eternal gain,
One day You're coming back and all will then be clear, it's true,
And in the meantime, we will trust, that's all we've left to do.

Gillian Humphries

WAR CORRESPONDENT

A genuine war correspondent
Is a true man of letters,
At war,
First and foremost.

He takes in all the experience,
Such horror
Of war
In his hands,
Warts and all,
As seen by him,
The full glory of violence
And human destruction,
Blood, sweat and tears.

He then puts it all in writing,
What he truly felt about it,
A war correspondent
Does just this
Only.

As a man of letters,
He writes brief and concise
Words of war,
The futility of war
As seen by him,
Warts and all.

A war correspondent
Never forgets
Such experiences.

John Floyd

UNTITLED

Standing alone in this dark room of time, what do I see?
Nothing but me,
I stand in the centre, waiting for what?
Waiting for something that I have not.
The colours are drab now, no rainbows, no sky,
is this what they meant when they told us that lie?
The bombs have all stopped now, silence prevails,
and then all I hear is the children's wails.
They cry in the darkness, 'What did we do wrong?
You told us this war would not go on long.'
Now there's nothing left. No man or no beast,
this planet was ours what a way to treat.
We had it all, but now it is gone, and mankind now perished
with all that we cherished.
All gone now, still here in darkness, no bright shining light,
all this because men just wanted to fight.

Pauline Jones

MRS PARKES' CELLAR

When I was a small boy of just two or three
I remember protesting around Mummy's knee
The siren was yowling somewhere down the street
To warn us they're coming to drop bombs like sleet

Should we go to Mrs Parkes' down her deep cellar
But she's often full and our mum didn't tell her
And it takes lots of time just to get through the gate
Though Mrs Parkes does make us tea while we wait

Mum says, 'It's under the power station tonight I do fear
Though it's right round the corner so run there like deer,'
A long breathless rush with my feet dragging ground
Mum holds baby Les in her other hand

And down concrete steps to a big boiler room
We wait out the night, chat and doze in the gloom
Mum wonders if Mrs Parkes' cellar is cheery
She doesn't like this place, says it's too eerie.

As bombs drop with thuds and the houses fall down
She thanks God she got the other kids out of town
Mum's crying with anger, 'Don't you bomb my home'
She's got a nice table she don't want to burn

That table saved her life birthing Les one bad raid
But she needn't have worried, that table was saved
And weary we trudged through the rubble back home
'Our house is still standing,' she smiled with a groan

'When we get inside I'll get down on my knee
And then I will make us a nice cup of tea'
We looked out the back door and that's when we saw
The row holding Mrs Parkes' house was no more

Our house was cracked up and the coal bin was broke
Windows we'll board up to keep out the smoke
And for years we still saw that big cellar filled in
With rubble and neighbours we thought of as kin

Ken Guy

LEAVING

Off Johnny, off you go lad
Will you ever come back, will you ever return?
Say goodbye to friends and family, fight well and don't be bad.

Off Johnny, off to face your fore
We'll listen to the wireless we'll wait for your word
It pains your mum; it'll grieve your dad when you go.

Off Johnny, off Johnny watch out for yoursel'
Keep your head down and we love you.
Cause it pains us to see you go; to that living hell.

Off Johnny, just listen to the quiet sky
You'll miss those English summers,
Those rainy nights.
We'll remember you, goodbye.

Paul Balm

OMAGH - TOWN IN TURMOIL

Laughter and joy on that August day
Parents out shopping, children at play.
A car was parked by the side of the road
No one thought it carried a deadly load.
Warning was given, information was passed
Someone got it wrong, sent people towards the blast.
On television that night, news flashed the shame
Omagh town and its people will never be the same.
Lots of victims injured, twenty-nine dead
What was it about? No one said
To plan something like this by a terrorist cell
May the Devil take them to his home in Hell.
Family and friends loved ones lost
It took so long for anyone to give a toss.
Why was Omagh picked on, what did they do?
Did not deserve this as far as anyone knew.
I felt sorrow and sadness, anger and fear
As the story unfolded, can't help but shed tears.
Can no one live in peace and harmony any more?
So sad it is for people to hide behind a door.

(God bless you Omagh for your faith)

Robert Henry

Soon It Will Be Too Late

In this time of men of might,
They think they know best without hindsight,
Us mere mortals, we have no choice,
Take to pen to hear our voice,
Throughout the world numbers galore,
Shout for peace, we don't want war.

Though numbers starve it's a disgrace,
So they watch from their high place,
Throughout the lands we hear the cry,
All colours, all creeds are asking why?
Around the world we all implore,
Shout for peace, we don't want war.

Throughout the world they die in number,
While those on high nightly slumber,
Across the seas and oceans wide,
You'll find all people side by side,
Around the world right to its core,
We'll shout for peace, we don't want war.

They have no worries in their safe surround,
While warring parties do abound,
Dividing the world, turning it upside down,
Destroying the beauty that's all around,
Over time just a forgotten place,
Forgotten memories without a face.

What will happen to this ravaged land?
No trees, no grass, just rocks and sand,
Holes and craters, shattered landscape,
No hiding place, nowhere to escape,
We mourn the loss of the ones we love,
As terror rains down from high above.

The loss of its beauty is hard to explain,
A barren wilderness, a blot, a stain,
A time will come with given grace,
To generate new life in this open space,
To cherish this land with love and care,
With peace and harmony for all to share.

Graham Burns